QUESTIONS EXPLORED

WHAT IS RACIAL BIAS?

by Tammy Gagne

BrightPoint Press

San Diego, CA

© 2023 BrightPoint Press
an imprint of ReferencePoint Press, Inc.
Printed in the United States

For more information, contact:
BrightPoint Press
PO Box 27779
San Diego, CA 92198
www.BrightPointPress.com

ALL RIGHTS RESERVED.

No part of this work covered by the copyright hereon may be reproduced or used in any form or by any means—graphic, electronic, or mechanical, including photocopying, recording, taping, web distribution, or information storage retrieval systems—without the written permission of the publisher.

Content Consultant: Christia Spears Brown, PhD, College of Arts & Sciences, University of Kentucky

---

LIBRARY OF CONGRESS CATALOGING-IN-PUBLICATION DATA

Names: Gagne, Tammy, author.
Title: What is racial bias? / by Tammy Gagne.
Description: San Diego, CA: BrightPoint Press, [2023] | Series: Questions explored | Includes bibliographical references and index. | Audience: Grades 7-9
Identifiers: LCCN 2022029130 (print) | LCCN 2022029131 (eBook) | ISBN 9781678205102 (hardcover) | ISBN 9781678205119 (pdf)
Subjects: LCSH: Race discrimination--Juvenile literature. | Racism--Juvenile literature.
Classification: LCC HT1521 .G26 2023 (print) | LCC HT1521 (eBook) | DDC 305.8--dc23/eng/20220701
LC record available at https://lccn.loc.gov/2022029130
LC eBook record available at https://lccn.loc.gov/2022029131

CONTENTS

AT A GLANCE	4
INTRODUCTION	6
LEARNING ABOUT RACIAL BIAS	
CHAPTER ONE	12
WHAT IS THE HISTORY OF RACIAL BIAS?	
CHAPTER TWO	30
HOW DOES RACIAL BIAS AFFECT INDIVIDUALS?	
CHAPTER THREE	44
HOW DOES RACIAL BIAS AFFECT SOCIETY?	
CHAPTER FOUR	58
WHAT CAN BE DONE TO PREVENT RACIAL BIAS?	
Glossary	74
Source Notes	75
For Further Research	76
Index	78
Image Credits	79
About the Author	80

AT A GLANCE

- Racial bias is an attitude or opinion that a person forms about other people based on their race. Bias can affect the way the person treats these people.

- Racial bias has been a problem in the United States for a long time. It is strongly linked to the practice of slavery. Since before the country's founding, white people in North America created harmful stereotypes about people of color.

- There are two types of racial bias. When a person is aware of her bias, it is called explicit bias. When a person is unaware of her bias, it is called implicit bias.

- Implicit bias can make people jump to conclusions about people of different races.

- Being a target of racial bias can be scary and frustrating. It can cause some people to develop physical and mental health problems.

- Racial bias affects both individuals and society. It is a problem in schools, workplaces, hospitals, and the justice system.

- Some police departments use racial profiling. Police officers who use racial profiling are more likely to suspect or stop people of color.

- People can reduce their racial bias. They can lessen its impact by talking about bias honestly, learning more about bias, and working to educate others. They can also practice empathy by looking at issues from different viewpoints.

INTRODUCTION

LEARNING ABOUT RACIAL BIAS

Megan and Gabby were on their way home from the movies. Gabby's brother Alex was driving them home. Alex was seventeen. He'd had his driver's license for about a year. He was a very responsible driver. He always made sure that everyone buckled their seatbelts.

Racial bias can sometimes lead police officers to be more suspicious of people of color.

They were all chatting happily about the movie. Suddenly, blue lights flashed behind them. Everyone stopped talking. Alex signaled and pulled over.

Racial bias can impact the way people treat others.

A police officer came up to the car. "License and registration," he said sternly. Alex handed him the documents. The officer looked at them and asked who the car belonged to. Alex started to explain that it was his stepfather's. But the officer cut him off. "The last names don't match," he snapped. "Your mother's boyfriend?" he asked. Alex repeated himself politely.

The officer asked if Alex had permission to take the car. Alex said he did. He calmly asked why the officer stopped him. But the officer raised his voice. He said driving under the speed limit was just as dangerous as speeding. Alex apologized.

"Don't argue with me, son," the officer snapped. "I'll let you go with a warning."

On the way home, an awkward silence filled the car. Finally, Megan broke it. She asked why the officer treated Alex so rudely. He told her it was likely because he was Black. It was probably the result of racial bias. This is an attitude or opinion that people form about others based on their race. Megan had heard of racial bias. But she had never seen it happen.

The conversation made Megan feel uncomfortable. She wondered if she had any racial biases. Alex said that everyone had some biases. "But talking about it like this is good," he said. "It helps keep us from letting racial bias affect how we treat others." Megan relaxed a bit. But she decided to learn more about bias. She never wanted to treat someone badly

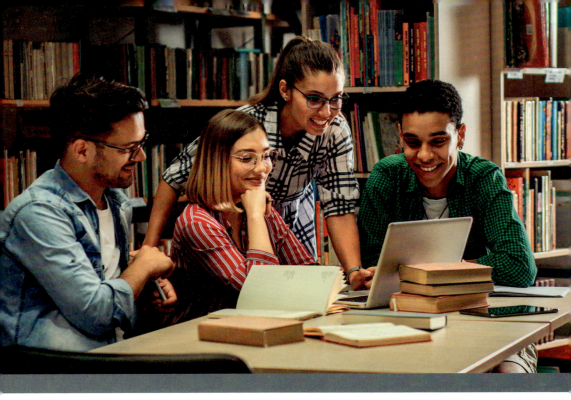

Learning more about racial bias is a good way to fight against it.

because of it. She planned to go to the library to look for books about racial bias. Alex even suggested a few titles. As they drove home, Megan felt more hopeful. She would work on overcoming any biases she had. She would be part of the solution.

CHAPTER ONE

WHAT IS THE HISTORY OF RACIAL BIAS?

Racial bias has existed for as long as the idea of race. The word *race* has been used since the 1500s. But back then, it meant "type" or "sort." In the late 1700s, the English started using the word to group people by **ancestry**. This was after they set up colonies in North America. The English

Westerns strengthened harmful stereotypes of Native Americans. This made many people form racial biases against Native people.

thought they were more civilized than the Native Americans. One reason for this was that the Native Americans looked different from the colonists. English colonists created

In the 2000s, people criticized sports teams for having racist Native-themed names and logos. In response, some teams, including the Cleveland Indians, changed their names.

stereotypes about Native people. They saw them as unintelligent and violent.

These stereotypes were passed down through generations. Even people who had never met a Native person believed these ideas. In the 1900s, people created books and movies called Westerns. These made the stereotypes even stronger. In these stories, Native Americans were shown as the enemies of white heroes. This made many people form racial biases against Native people.

During the same time, many sports team owners gave their teams Native-themed names. This added to racial bias against Native Americans. People thought the names sounded fierce. Team logos often included images of violent Native Americans. In the 2000s, a growing number of people began criticizing this practice.

They called the names and logos **racist**.
Some teams changed their names. For
example, the Cleveland Indians became the
Cleveland Guardians in 2021. But the teams
still inspired racial biases for decades. And
these biases live on.

BIAS AGAINST BLACK PEOPLE

Beginning in the 1600s, white settlers in
what is now the United States practiced
slavery. Europeans kidnapped large
numbers of African people. They brought
them to the colonies in chains. Then they
sold the African people to colonists. The
colonists saw enslaved people as property.

Slavery was a common practice in the American colonies. Enslaved people were forced to do difficult jobs like farming and harvesting crops.

They treated them harshly. They forced them to do difficult jobs, such as farming. They made the enslaved people work for free. This way, the white people could make more money. They could get richer while doing little work themselves. Slavery was most common in the South. But by 1750,

The colonists treated enslaved people like property. They believed that people with darker skin were worth less than people with white skin.

it was legal in all the colonies. The practice existed for over two hundred years.

The colonists' idea of race was closely tied to the slave trade. Many white people had negative beliefs about African people. They used these beliefs to justify their treatment of Africans. White people thought white skin was better than darker skin. They thought the Africans' skin color made them worth less than white people.

The colonists depended on slave labor. They relied on it to grow and harvest crops. They also used the Africans for other jobs, such as making tools. White people often used violence to make the Africans obey them. They saw them as a group that needed to be controlled. In 2019, the *Journal of Human Rights and Social Work* published an article about the colonists' stereotypes. It states, "Their strong stereotypical beliefs governed how African-Americans were to be treated, never as individuals, but always collectively. . . . Even after slavery was abolished, the standards for treatment of African-Americans remained the same."[1] In 1865, the Thirteenth Amendment to the US Constitution was passed. This finally outlawed slavery.

THE TREATMENT OF CHINESE IMMIGRANTS

In the mid-1800s, new technology was changing the United States. Workers built a railroad. It would carry people across the

In the mid-1800s, thousands of Chinese immigrants worked to build railroads. Many Americans discriminated against these workers because of their race.

continent. Racial biases continued to be part of society. And they were not limited to African Americans and Native Americans. Most railroad workers were immigrants. Between 1863 and 1869, as many as 20,000 Chinese immigrants worked on the railroad. They worked for the Central Pacific Railroad. They shoveled heavy rocks for up to twelve hours a day. This made room for the rails.

Many Americans formed racial biases against Chinese immigrants. Americans saw them as outsiders. They did not think the new workers belonged in the United States. Many of the other railroad workers used racist **slurs** for the Chinese people. Even the railroad company treated them poorly. Chinese workers were paid less than others for the same jobs. They were not given meals or shelter like other workers.

Many Chinese workers even slept in the underground tunnels where they worked. Chris Lu was US deputy secretary of labor from 2014 to 2017. In 2021, he said, "We'll never know the names of most of

US-VERSUS-THEM THINKING

In the 1990s, Madeleine Albright was US secretary of state. She had strong opinions about bias. She thought too many Americans saw people who were unlike them as rivals. They did not think about how differences can be good. Instead, they saw these people as competition. They worried about competing with them for education, jobs, or housing. Albright called this an "us-versus-them" way of thinking. She thought it made bias a bigger problem.

The Chinese Exclusion Act banned Chinese immigrants from coming to the United States. It also kept Chinese people who were already in the country from becoming US citizens.

these Chinese workers, but their sacrifices were responsible for one of the greatest engineering feats in U.S. history."[2]

The railroad was finished in 1869. But racial bias against Chinese people continued. The US government passed laws that **discriminated** against Chinese people. In 1882, the Chinese Exclusion Act was passed. This banned new Chinese workers from coming to the United States. It also prevented Chinese immigrants from becoming US citizens. This kept them from having rights such as voting rights. Americans wanted to keep Chinese people from settling in the nation. These racist attitudes affected their actions.

EXPLICIT AND IMPLICIT RACIAL BIAS

Some people are aware of their racial biases. This type of bias is called

People with explicit biases believe stereotypes about people of other races. They often think their biases are justified.

explicit bias. People with explicit biases may believe that stereotypes about people of color are true. For example, a person might see a movie that features a violent Black person. After the movie, the person may start to believe the stereotype that

Black people are dangerous. A person with explicit bias thinks his opinions are justified. This is true even when he takes a second look at his bias.

Sometimes people are unaware that they have a racial bias. This is called implicit bias. A person with implicit bias may not really believe one racial group is more dangerous than another. But she may still have biases that impact her actions. She might not realize she has these biases. The bias is not intentional. But it can still be harmful.

Some police officers have implicit biases against Black people. This can make them jump to conclusions. For example, an officer may see a Black person holding an object from far away. He might assume the object is a weapon. In more than 100 cases since 2015, police officers have shot and killed unarmed Black people.

BIAS AND DISCRIMINATION

Racial bias and discrimination are related. But they are not the same thing. Racial bias is a belief about a certain race. Discrimination happens when someone acts on that belief. For example, a restaurant manager may have implicit bias against her Black employees. Because of this, she might choose not to hire a Black worker who is qualified for a job. If that happens, it is discrimination.

A person with implicit bias is unaware of his bias. This can make him jump to conclusions about people of color.

Both explicit and implicit bias are problems in modern society. They can lead to stereotypes, racism, and discrimination. But people can lessen the impact of racial bias. They can work to prevent it in both individuals and society. A great way to start is by understanding how racial bias works.

CHAPTER TWO

HOW DOES RACIAL BIAS AFFECT INDIVIDUALS?

Implicit bias can affect how people treat others. White people with implicit biases may be less friendly toward people of color. They might avoid smiling or making eye contact. They may even choose to sit farther away from people of color.

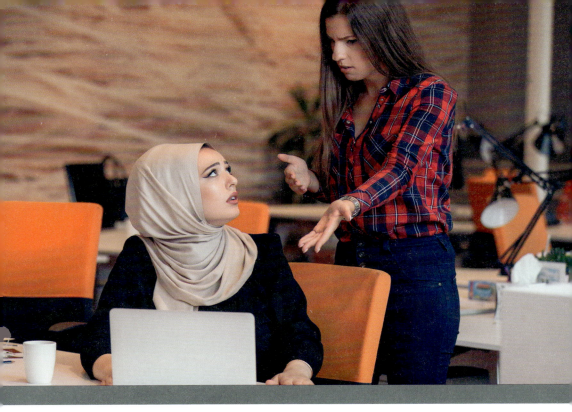

People with implicit biases may act less friendly toward people of other races.

Implicit bias can also make people jump to conclusions. This may happen when people of different races get into an argument. Some people believe a stereotype that Black people are angry or threatening. A person with implicit bias

People with implicit bias may make assumptions about a person of color's abilities.

might assume a Black person started the fight.

School or work projects can also show implicit bias. White partners may assume that people of other races are not as good at certain tasks. Rachel Godsil is a law professor. She studies implicit bias.

She said that people with implicit biases often perform poorly when working with people of color. She said, "Without knowing it, they were challenged mentally by the effort of appearing non-biased."[3]

EFFECTS ON MENTAL HEALTH

Experiencing racial bias can be **traumatic**. Sometimes it can even lead to mental health problems. People who experience racism may suffer from depression or anxiety disorders. Some may even develop **post-traumatic stress disorder (PTSD)**. They may also develop substance use disorders or suicidal thoughts.

Experiencing racial bias can negatively impact a person's mental health.

Being a target of bias can be frightening and frustrating. For example, a person with bias may use hateful language toward people of color. A person with bias might also treat others unfairly through his actions. A student may need a teacher's permission to take an advanced class. A teacher with bias might assume that a Black student cannot handle the class. This is unfair to the student. Situations like these negatively affect people of color. They could even cause people to develop mental health issues.

THE EFFECTS OF ONGOING RACISM

A 2020 study looked at how racism impacts mental health. It found that racism led to depression in Black teens. Earlier studies showed similar results. But this study paid special attention to how often teens experienced racism. Many of the teens were repeated targets of racism. Their depression got worse over time. These results showed that ongoing racism can lead to more serious mental health problems.

A person does not need to experience racial bias firsthand to feel its effects. Seeing racism can be enough to cause mental trauma. For instance, it might be traumatic to watch a news video of police mistreating a Black person.

EFFECTS ON PHYSICAL HEALTH

Racial bias can cause stress. This affects both the mind and body. A 2020 survey looked at Americans' stress levels. It found that 67 percent of Black Americans feel stress from discrimination. This stress can lead to many physical health problems. These include high blood pressure, heart

Seeing racism happen to others can be enough to cause mental trauma.

disease, and diabetes. Sometimes this stress can also cause people to cope with their feelings in unhealthy ways.

Professor Anthony Ong studies human development. In 2017, he led

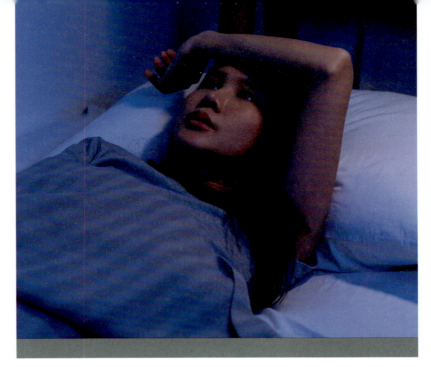

People who experience microaggressions may have trouble getting enough sleep.

a study. It followed 152 Asian American college students. Ong wanted to learn how microaggressions affected sleep. Microaggressions are words or actions that show bias in indirect ways. Many microaggressions come from stereotypes. For example, a white person might compliment an Asian person on her English. In this situation, the white person assumes the Asian person was not born in the United States.

The study showed that microaggressions negatively affect sleep. After students experienced a microaggression, they slept fewer hours at night. They also slept poorly. Not getting enough sleep is linked to many health problems. These include heart disease, strokes, and kidney disease.

Sometimes people express microaggressions without even realizing it. But this is still harmful. Kevin Nadal is a psychology professor. He pointed out that everyone makes mistakes sometimes. Nadal said, "It's not necessarily that you're a bad person if you commit a microaggression, but rather that you need to be more aware of your biases and impact on people."[4]

HOW RACIAL BIAS CAN AFFECT HEALTH CARE

Racial bias can even affect health care. It can impact how doctors treat their patients. Research shows that people of color generally receive worse health care than white people. In 2020, Amy Mason-Cooley

Racial bias can impact how doctors treat their patients. A doctor with racial bias might dismiss a person of color's concerns.

went to the emergency room. She has

sickle cell disease. This illness can cause

great pain. But her doctor refused to give

her medication for it. He assumed she was

an **addicted** person looking for drugs. Mason-Cooley felt like the doctor was not listening to her. She asked for a different doctor. But he laughed at her. She felt judged and dismissed.

Sevon Blake had a similar experience. She was having stomach pain. But her doctor kept telling her she was fine. So Blake decided to change doctors. She said, "I didn't feel like I could talk to my previous doctor, if he was just going to dismiss me." She ended up seeing a Black female doctor. This doctor told Blake that she had gluten intolerance. This illness makes it hard to digest some foods. Blake just needed to follow a specific diet. If her first doctor had listened to her, she could have found relief sooner.

PAINFUL BIASES

Racial bias can keep people from getting the right treatment for pain. One study looked at the biases of medical students. It found that 40 percent of medical students believe Black people have thicker skin than white people. Because of this, the students assumed Black people were less sensitive to pain. Another study looked at Black and white patients with painful medical conditions. Doctors were 22 percent less likely to give pain medication to the Black patients.

CHAPTER THREE

HOW DOES RACIAL BIAS AFFECT SOCIETY?

R acial bias not only impacts individuals. It also impacts society. It can affect the way people behave at work, school, or other social spaces. Sometimes, people in positions of power even let bias affect their actions and decisions.

Racial bias can influence how people behave in social settings.

This can have harmful consequences for many people.

RACIAL BIAS IN SCHOOLS

School is often one of the first places people experience racial bias. Many people think teachers are fair-minded. But this

Some teachers let racial bias impact how they treat Black students.

is not always true. Jordan Starck studies psychology at Princeton University. In 2020, he led a study about teachers and racial bias. He said, "Teachers are probably more well-intentioned than the general population, but they still have the same bias levels."[5]

Some teachers let bias affect their teaching. Starck found that white teachers often treat Black students differently. Many teachers have lower expectations of Black students. They do not work as hard to teach those students difficult concepts. They are also less likely to place Black students in gifted education classes. This can affect how many Black students graduate high school or go to college.

Teachers are not the only people in schools with racial bias. Students have biases too. They may learn these from the media, other kids, or other adults.

Kids often learn racial biases from their parents, the media, or their peers. These biases can affect how they behave toward others.

Many kids learn racial biases from their parents. This is not always intentional. But sometimes parents pass biases on to their children. And these biases can affect their children's behavior.

Nathaniel K. Jones is a doctor. He still remembers a day from his childhood. He and his friends were pretending to be *Star Wars* characters. His friends told him that he could not be Han Solo because Solo was white. They said he had to be Lando,

RACIAL BIAS IN THE NEWS

US news outlets often share stories about white people who go missing. Many of these stories are shown on national television. They make it easier for police to find missing people. But news outlets are less likely to share stories about missing people of color. This makes it harder to find those people. Racial bias in the news can affect viewers too. Viewers may think that the lives of people of color are less important than the lives of white people.

a Black character. When Nathaniel got home, his mother told him about racism. He said, "She explained that just because we thought race didn't matter in our family, that didn't protect us from how much it matters to the world around us."[6]

RACIAL BIAS IN THE WORKPLACE

Racial bias impacts the workplace too. Some white people in positions of power let biases affect their hiring decisions. For example, a job application might list a name that sounds like it belongs to a person of color. A manager with racial bias might choose to ignore that application.

Some people might let racial biases affect who they choose to hire for a job.

Other managers may not promote people of color who already work for the company. This makes it hard for those people to succeed.

Other types of bias also happen in the workplace. Nearly half of Black and Latina women have experienced a specific microaggression. People assume they have lower job positions, such as administrative assistants or custodians. Racial bias makes these people think that women of color cannot hold higher positions.

Racist behavior can happen in all kinds of work settings. For example, a Black nurse experienced racial bias when she entered a white patient's room. The patient was surprised that the Black woman was a nurse. She asked about the nurse's education and experience.

Later, the nurse's boss assigned someone else to the patient. The patient

Many Black and Latina women experience microaggressions in the workplace. People assume they hold low-level positions.

said the Black nurse was not a good fit. Her removal from the case had nothing to do with her abilities. But the patient's racial bias made the nurse question herself. She felt sick to her stomach and started to wonder if she should even be a nurse.

Police officers often treat people of color differently than white people. Black people are much more likely to be unfairly stopped by the police.

RACIAL BIAS IN LEGAL SETTINGS

Racial bias also affects the legal system. When it comes to the law, people of color are often treated differently than white people. For example, Black people have different experiences with police.

Black people are about five times more likely to report being unfairly stopped. Police are trained to look for suspicious activity. But some officers let bias affect their behavior. They may be more suspicious of Black people.

RACIAL PROFILING

Some police departments use racial profiling. This means they target people of color for certain crimes. They do this because of bias. They believe people of color are more likely to commit crimes. Police who use racial profiling are more likely to stop Hispanic people. They check whether the people are in the United States legally. Many law experts say racial profiling goes against the US Constitution. But the practice is still a problem.

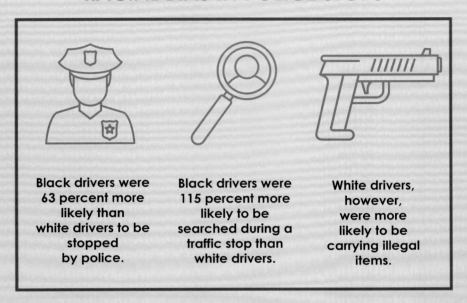

A study of police stops in North Carolina showed that Black drivers were much more likely to be stopped and searched by police than white drivers.

This unfair treatment continues after a person of color is arrested. Courts often make deals with people accused of crimes. These are called plea bargains. These deals

Black people are less likely to be offered plea bargains than white people. They often get longer prison sentences than white people who have committed the same crime.

offer lighter sentences when people agree to plead guilty. But Black people are less likely than white people to be offered plea bargains. They are also more likely to serve longer, harsher sentences than white people. This is true even when they have committed the same crime.

CHAPTER FOUR

WHAT CAN BE DONE TO PREVENT RACIAL BIAS?

There are many things people can do to prevent racial bias. Raising awareness is a good first step. People can learn more about racial bias. This can help keep bias from affecting their behavior. But many experts think it is impossible to

Being more aware of racial bias can help keep it from affecting a person's behavior.

stop bias completely. Jennifer Eberhardt is a psychology professor. She wrote a book about racial bias. She said, "Bias is not something we cure, it's something we manage. There's no magical moment where bias just ends and we never have to deal with it again."[7]

SEEKING HELP FOR RACIAL BIAS

Victims of racial bias may not know what to do about it. Some biased behaviors are hard to prove. Others are clear acts of discrimination or racism. It is illegal to harass people because of their race. This should be reported to a teacher, principal, or police officer.

A victim of racial bias may feel distrustful of others. He may be scared of biased behavior happening again. He might also have trouble controlling his emotions. These are all normal responses to racial trauma. Experts say that victims should share these

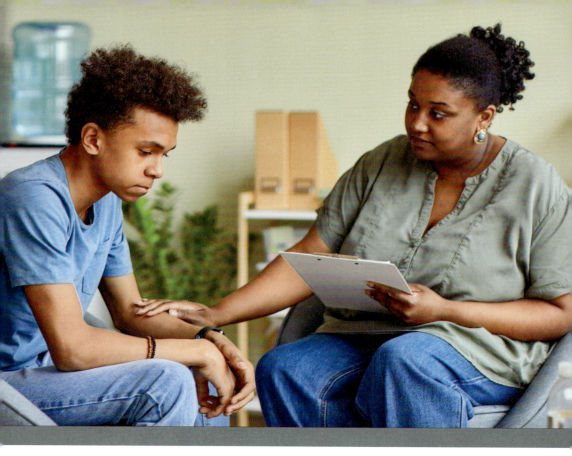

It can be helpful for victims of racial bias to talk to friends, family, or mental health professionals.

feelings with others. Talking to family and friends can help. It may also be helpful to talk to a mental health professional.

It can be healthy to acknowledge feelings such as anger. It can help a person manage

Many victims of racism are inspired to become part of the solution. They join protests, raise awareness, and help educate others about bias.

her feelings. Talking about anger can also help a person use it positively. Many victims of racism decide to become part of the solution. Some join protests. Others educate people about racial bias.

News stories about racial bias can be hard to read or watch. They often stir up difficult feelings or memories. This is especially true for victims of racial bias. Some people call this being triggered. A trigger is something that negatively affects a person's mental state. In this situation, it can be helpful to take a break from television and social media. Watching the news or reading articles can make trauma worse. Limiting the amount of time spent with the news can provide relief.

REDUCING ONE'S OWN RACIAL BIAS

Humans create habits easily. People naturally try to find patterns in life. In many situations, it is helpful to know what to expect. The brain constantly takes in information for this purpose. This is how implicit bias develops. The human brain also tends to take shortcuts. This makes it easier for a person to process information. People often rely on past experiences when forming thoughts and opinions. These experiences do not have to be firsthand. Sometimes they come from books, movies, or news stories. It does not matter how

News stories involving racism can stir up difficult memories for victims of racial bias. It can be helpful to take a break from the news.

truthful the information is either. All these things affect people's biases.

Experts say that people should slow down when they feel threatened or scared. This is often when their biases can affect

Empathy can help a person better understand how victims of discrimination might feel.

their behavior. In many cases, being aware of bias can stop a person from acting on it. Taking time to think before acting can also help. It allows people to think more clearly. It reminds them to consider all sides of an issue.

Another way to reduce bias is by practicing empathy. This means thinking about a situation from another person's viewpoint. Empathy helps someone understand another person's feelings. It makes him think about how a person experiencing discrimination might feel.

RACIAL BIAS EDUCATION

Talking about racial bias can be uncomfortable. But if people do not talk about it, it can make the problem worse. Education can help. Students, businesspeople, and police all need to learn about racial bias. This way, they can work

Education can help people of all ages learn more about racial bias. It can make people more aware of the issue, inspiring them to fight against it.

together to reduce it. Awareness is a good first step. But awareness alone cannot solve the problem. People must also learn ways to manage bias.

Racial bias will not just disappear. It is important to learn how to fight against it.

The University of Wisconsin created a training program for this. It teaches people how to overcome bias. People begin by taking a test. This test identifies biases. Then, people talk about stereotypes and ways to break those stereotypes. They are

SETTING BUSINESSES UP FOR SUCCESS

Diversity can help fight against racial bias. Businesses can put people of color in positions of power. By doing this, they show that equality matters. A diverse group of employees can have discussions about racial bias. They can help create new policies for the workplace. This can help a company become more aware of its own biases. It can keep bias from affecting how the company does business.

encouraged to interact more with different types of people. Francesca Gino and Katherine Coffman are professors. They study human behavior and stereotypes. They discussed the program in a *Harvard Business Review* article. They explained that the program's strategies work best when they become habits. "The more they're practiced, the more effective they will be," they said.[8]

Thinking and talking about bias can help reduce it. For example, a person can write about her biases in a journal. She might write about life experiences that

Talking about bias and listening to other people's experiences is a great way to learn about different perspectives.

may have shaped her biases. She might also try looking at those experiences from other viewpoints. It might help to talk about biases with friends too. Listening to other

By working together, people can prevent racial bias and reduce its power over society.

people's experiences is a great way to learn about different perspectives.

Everyone has some racial biases. But by working together, people can fight against them. They can help make sure that biases do not affect the way they treat others. They can learn more about bias and work to prevent it. They can educate others about racial bias. This can help reduce its power over individuals and society.

TAKING ACTION

Anyone can make a difference. The person does not have to be an expert or a mental health professional. Zoë Jenkins was a high school senior in Lexington, Kentucky. She saw a need for racial bias education at her school. In 2020, Zoë designed an online antibias training program for students. She worked with the University of Kentucky. Together, they made the fourteen-week program free for everyone.

GLOSSARY

addicted
dependent on a substance such as drugs

ancestry
a person's family history going back many generations

discriminated
treated unfairly because of race, gender, or other factors

diversity
the inclusion of individuals from different races, genders, and other groups

post-traumatic stress disorder (PTSD)
a mental illness caused by severe trauma

racist
based on the belief that one's own race is better than another

slurs
insulting names for a particular group of people

stereotypes
oversimplified beliefs about a group of people

traumatic
causing mental or emotional pain or injury

SOURCE NOTES

CHAPTER ONE: WHAT IS THE HISTORY OF RACIAL BIAS?

1. Quoted in Evi Taylor, et al, "The Historical Perspectives of Stereotypes," *Journal of Human Rights and Social Work*, vol. 4, May 7, 2019, pp. 1–13.

2. Quoted in Ray Rogers, "What Can the Transcontinental Railroad Teach Us?" *National Geographic*, May 17, 2021. www.nationalgeographic.com.

CHAPTER TWO: HOW DOES RACIAL BIAS AFFECT INDIVIDUALS?

3. Quoted in Hayley Roberts, "Implicit Bias," *Open Society Foundations*, December 17, 2011. www.opensocietyfoundations.org.

4. Quoted in Andrew Limbong, "Microaggressions Are a Big Deal," *NPR*, June 9, 2020. www.npr.org.

CHAPTER THREE: HOW DOES RACIAL BIAS AFFECT SOCIETY?

5. Quoted in Madeline Will, "Teachers Are as Racially Biased as Everybody Else," *Education Week*, June 9, 2020. www.edweek.org.

6. Nathaniel K. Jones, "Learning About Racism," *American Academy of Pediatrics*, July 29, 2019. www.aap.org.

CHAPTER FOUR: WHAT CAN BE DONE TO PREVENT RACIAL BIAS?

7. Quoted in Ailsa Chang, "Can We Overcome Racial Bias?" *NPR*, March 28, 2019. www.npr.org.

8. Francesca Gino and Katherine Coffman, "Unconscious Bias Training That Works," *Harvard Business Review*, September–October 2021. https://hbr.org.

FOR FURTHER RESEARCH

BOOKS

Mary Boone, *Racial Injustice*. San Diego, CA: BrightPoint Press, 2023.

Duchess Harris, JD, PhD, with Tammy Gagne, *Race and the Media in Modern America*. Minneapolis, MN: Abdo Publishing, 2021.

Duchess Harris, JD, PhD, with R. L. Van, *Race and Policing in Modern America*. Minneapolis, MN: Abdo Publishing, 2021.

INTERNET SOURCES

Vanessa Bhimanprommachak, "How to Call Out Your Friend for a Racist Comment," *Harvard Business Review*, August 24, 2021. https://hbr.org.

Bethany Brookshire, "Suffering from Racist Acts Can Prompt Black Teens to Constructive Action," *Science News for Students*, December 7, 2020. www.snexplores.org.

"How to Support People from Different Cultural Backgrounds," *ReachOut*, n.d. https://au.reachout.com.

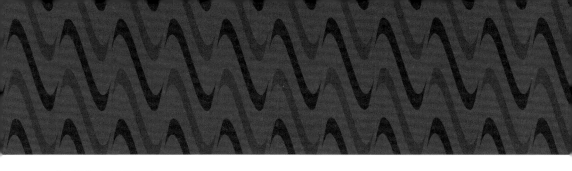

WEBSITES

American Civil Liberties Union (ACLU)
www.aclu.org

The ACLU is an organization that defends and preserves the constitutional rights and liberties of everyone in the United States.

Color of Change
https://colorofchange.org

Color of Change is an online racial justice organization. It works with corporations and governments to create a less hostile world for Black people in America.

The Leadership Conference on Civil and Human Rights
https://civilrights.org

The Leadership Conference on Civil and Human Rights works for civil rights legislation in the United States.

INDEX

Albright, Madeleine, 23
awareness, 25, 40, 58, 66, 68, 69

Black Americans, 10, 16–20, 26–28, 31–32, 35, 36, 42, 43, 47, 50, 51–53, 54–57
Blake, Sevon, 42–43

Chinese Exclusion Act, 25
Chinese immigrants, 20–25

discrimination, 25, 28, 29, 36, 60, 67
diversity, 69

Eberhardt, Jennifer, 59
empathy, 67
explicit bias, 25–27, 29

health care, 40–43

implicit bias, 27–29, 30–33, 64

Jones, Nathaniel K., 49–50

legal system, 54–57
Lu, Chris, 23–24

Mason-Cooley, Amy, 41–42
mental health, 33–37, 60–63
microaggressions, 38–40, 51–52

Native Americans, 13–16, 21

Ong, Anthony, 37–38

perspectives, 67, 71–72
physical health, 36–37, 39, 41–43
plea bargains, 56–57
police, 27–28, 36, 49, 54–55, 56, 60, 67
police stops, 55, 56
post-traumatic stress disorder (PTSD), 33
prison sentences, 56–57

race, 10, 12, 18–19, 28, 31, 32–33, 50, 60
racial bias education, 11, 58, 63, 68–73
racial profiling, 55
racism, 15–16, 18–19, 22, 25, 29, 33–37, 50, 52, 60, 62–63

schools, 32–33, 44, 45–48, 73
slavery, 16–20
Starck, Jordan, 46
stereotypes, 14–15, 19–20, 26–28, 29, 31–32, 38–39, 69–70
stress, 36–37

teachers, 34–35, 45–47, 60
Thirteenth Amendment, 20
trauma, 33, 36–37, 60, 63

us-versus-them thinking, 23

Westerns, 14–15
workplaces, 50–53

IMAGE CREDITS

Cover: © Roman Chazov/
Shutterstock Images
5: © Motortion Films/
Shutterstock Images
7: © Frame Stock Footage/
Shutterstock Images
8: © Lord Henri Voton/iStockphoto
11: © Zoran Zeremski/
Shutterstock Images
13: © Shawshots/Alamy
14: © Keeton Gale/
Shutterstock Images
17: © Everett Collection/
Shutterstock Images
18: © Duncan 1890/iStockphoto
21: © Everett Collection/
Shutterstock Images
24: © Bauhaus 1000/iStockphoto
26: © Yakobchuk Viacheslav/
Shutterstock Images
29: © RYO Alexandre/
Shutterstock Images
31: © FS Stock/Shutterstock Images
32: © The Faces/Shutterstock Images
34: © Daisy-Daisy/iStockphoto
37: © Ringo Chiu/Shutterstock Images
38: © Kmpzzz/Shutterstock Images
41: © Monkey Business Images/
Shutterstock Images

45: © Fertnig/iStockphoto
46: © Skynesher/iStockphoto
48: © Zinkevych/iStockphoto
51: © Motortion Films/
Shutterstock Images
53: © Dario Gaona/iStockphoto
54: © Chameleons Eye/
Shutterstock Images
56: © Anatolir/Shutterstock Images
57: © Sir Travel a Lot/
Shutterstock Images
59: © Seventy-Four/
Shutterstock Images
61: © Seventy-Four/
Shutterstock Images
62: © Diego G. Diaz/
Shutterstock Images
65: © Lia Russy/Shutterstock Images
66: © Monkey Business Images/
iStockphoto
68: © Monkey Business Images/
Shutterstock Images
71: © Olena Yakobchuk/
Shutterstock Images
72: © Sheila Fitzgerald/
Shutterstock Images

ABOUT THE AUTHOR

Tammy Gagne has written hundreds of books for both adults and children. Some of her recent books have been about gaming disorder and media bias. She lives in northern New England with her husband, son, and dogs.